ANUSHKA SEN – THE UNTOLD STORY

SUSHANT MASIH

Copyright © Sushant Masih
All Rights Reserved.

This book has been published with all efforts taken to make the material error-free after the consent of the author. However, the author and the publisher do not assume and hereby disclaim any liability to any party for any loss, damage, or disruption caused by errors or omissions, whether such errors or omissions result from negligence, accident, or any other cause.

While every effort has been made to avoid any mistake or omission, this publication is being sold on the condition and understanding that neither the author nor the publishers or printers would be liable in any manner to any person by reason of any mistake or omission in this publication or for any action taken or omitted to be taken or advice rendered or accepted on the basis of this work. For any defect in printing or binding the publishers will be liable only to replace the defective copy by another copy of this work then available.

Contents

ANUSHKA SEN

CHAPTER ONE

ANUSHKA SEN - THE UNTOLD STORY

This Story covers a detailed story about the Indian Television actress & Model Anushka Sen. It Covers more details about Anushka Sen's age, Early Life, Body measurement, Career, Caste, Affairs, Siblings, Family, Net Worth, boyfriend, Photos, About, Movie list, Show list, serials list, Facebook, Instagram, Twitter, Youtube Channel, Net Worth, Salary, Facts, Occupation, Profession, Education, Education Qualification, Achievements, Awards, Photos, Videos, Gossips, News, Career & more.

ANUSHKA SEN

[3:42 PM, 6/24/2022] sushant: Being good in her studies, Anushka passed her high school examination with a good number. She had scored 89.4% in her 12th board examination. She did her High School and Senior Secondary at Ryan International School, Kandivali, Mumbai.

Anushka takes admission to Thakur College of Science and Commerce, Mumbai to pursue a degree in filmography and to learn and enhance the art of acting in films. She is active in the entertainment industry since childhood.

When she was just 7 years old, she got a chance to play the role of Misty in the serial Yahaan Main Ghar Ghar Kheli. After this, in the year 2011, she was got an opportunity to play Child Parvati in the famous Life OK show Devon Ke Dev ... Mahadev, based on mythology.

After this, in the year 2012, she played an episodic role in the horror story serial Fear Files: Darr Ki Sacchi Tasvirein. Then the same year started the SAB TV show Baalveer which is the most popular show among children for a long time.

In this show, Anushka played the lead role of Meher Dagli / Bal Sakhi which was highly appreciated by the TV audience. The show broke many TRP records and was in the top 10 in the TRP list at all times.

Anushka was very famous with this show, and her role in the show was well received. Despite being telecast for a full 4 years, the demand for the show increased so much that the makers had to decide that they launched the second season of Baalveer.
[3:42 PM, 6/24/2022] sushant: In 2013, she also participated in Comedy Circus's Mahabali. Anushka, who won millions of hearts with her acting in TV serials, got a chance to work as a child

actress in the Bollywood film Crazy Cukkad Family, released in 2015.

She also made her Bollywood debut with the film and in 2016, she appeared as a guest on another comedy show Comedy Nights Bachao Tazaa. She appeared in the year 2018 in the TV serial Internet Wala Love as Diya Verma.

After this, in 2019, she played the main role of Manikarnika Rao / Rani Laxmibai in the Zee TV serial Jhansi Ki Rani. This TV serial was well received by the audience and won millions of hearts with her acting.

She was also seen in the year 2019 in a music video Gal Karke opposite Siddharth Nigam. Anushka was seen in the role of Rani Singh Rajawat in another serial Apna Time Bhi Aayega in the year 2020, but later she left the serial in the middle due to her health issues.

However, in the same year 2020, she appeared in three consecutive videos Superstar, Pyar Naal, and Aaina. This year in 2021, she is going to be seen as a contestant in Colors TV's most popular show Fear Factor: Khatron Khiladi.

The show is being shot in Cape Town, and will soon be aired on Colors TV after the shooting is over. Apart from Anushka Sen, many big TV actors like Rahul Vaidya, Shweta Tiwari, Mehak Chahal, Divyanka Tripathi Dahiya, Arjun Bijlani, and Saurabh Raj Jain are also participating in the show as a contestant

Famous Bollywood action director Rohit Shetty is scheduled to host the 11th season of Fear Factor. Earlier in 2021, Anushka has appeared in the role of Alia in ZEE 5 Alt Balaji's web series Crashh

Anushka Sen's age is just 19 years old in 2022. She is the youngest artist in the Hindi TV industry. Her physical appearance is amazing, which is very beautiful in appearance.

She also pays great attention to her fitness so that her body can look attractive. She resorts to yoga and gym daily to keep herself fit. She used to eat green vegetables and fruit juice daily to keep her body healthy so that her body can remain healthy.

Anushka Sen's height is 5 feet 4 inches, which is 163 cm. Her bodyweight is 48 kg and Anushka's body measurement is 34-23-32. Her eye color is black and her hair color is Black.

Anushka was born into a small Hindu family in Jharkhand. A few days after her birth, her entire family shifted from Jharkhand to Mumbai. Being born into a Hindu family, she worships Hindu deities from the beginning and adheres to Hindu customs, besides respecting all religions.

Anushka is very close to her father Anirban Sen who supports her every decision. Anushka is also very close to her mother Rajarupa Sen. She keeps sharing the latest photos on social media on the day she comes with her mother. Anushka is the only child of her parents and has no siblings.

Talking about her marital status, she is still unmarried and she is not having an affair with any boy. She is just a young 18-year-old actress who is completely dedicated to her work and aspires to achieve a new place in the field of acting.

Talking about Anushka Sharma's total net worth, she has achieved a different position on her acting at a young age. She charges around ?1 lakh for an episode of TV serials. Their total net worth ranges from around ?15 crores. She also owns a blue BMW 330I M Sports Limited Edition car.

Her main sources of earning are TV serials, music videos, films, and web series and apart from that she also earns a lot of money from TV commercial aids. She promotes the products of many brands through her Instagram and also shares some sponsor posts with which she makes money.

In the year 2021, she has gone to Cape Town to participate in Colors TV's popular show Fear Factor Khatron Ke Khiladi, where she is charging around ?5 lakh for each episode.

Talking about Anushka's favorite things, her favorites are Bollywood actors Ranveer Singh and Ishaan Khattar and her favorite actress is Kangana Ranaut. Anushka is very fond of food, with Kadhi Chawal and Palak Paneer being her favorite dishes.

Her hobbies like Dancing, Shopping, Traveling, Playing Guitar & Harmonium. Anushka loves Bollywood movies with her favorite film Kangana Ranaut's Queen which was released in 2013. In the table below, we have given a list of all their favorite things, which you must read once.

Anushka Sen's account is present on all social media platforms where she keeps giving the latest updates to her fans about her TV serial music videos web series and movies. She is very active on Instagram where her posts number up to 4.1k and she is followed by more than 18.5 million followers. Watch Anushka Sen's Instagram stories anonymously.

She is also very active on Facebook where she has more than 6.6 million followers. Anushka's account is also on Twitter where she has more than 74.4k followers. She keeps her followers updated by tweeting through her Twitter handle.

Apart from this, she also has her own channel on YouTube which has around 2.12 million subscribers. She keeps uploading her music videos, promotional videos, and fitness-related videos to her subscribers on YouTube.

She is also present on Wikipedia's page, where you can read about them in detail. Anushka is also the brand ambassador of the Likee app, her Likee app username is @anushkasen_04. In the table below, we have shared all the links of her social media account with you, by clicking on which you will be able to directly access her profile page

Some Interesting Fact About Anushka Sen:
Anushka Sen is a famous child artist of a Hindi Tv serial.
She is an Indian model & actress.

She did complete her school at Ryan International School,
Kandivali, Mumbai, India.
Anushka also got an award in her school.

She got immense popularity from the tv show Balveer and Jhansi
Ki Rani.
She made her debut in the television serial Yahaan Main Ghar Ghar
Kheli which was released in 2009, at the age of 7.
She is also a pet dog lover.

Anushka is also a trained dancer and got trained from Shiamak
Davar Dance Academy.
She loves to play guitar and piano in her spare time.

She also appeared in many Music videos like 'Gal Karke' (2018),
'Viah' (2018), and 'Superstar' (2020).

She appeared in various TV shoots and brand advertisements like Orient with Former Indian Captain Ms Dhoni.

Anushka Sen in Orient tv ads with Mahendra Singh Dhoni
Anushka is a brand ambassador of the Likee app.
She likes traveling and shopping as well as Dancing.
Anushka also appeared in the short movie Sammaditthi in 2019.

She worships Hindu deities and believes in Hindu culture.

FAQ On Anushka Sen:
Que. In which class is Anushka Sen?
Ans. Anushka passed her 10th and 12th board exams with good numbers. Now, She is currently pursuing filmography from Thakur College of Commerce & Arts, Mumbai.

Que. What happened to Anushka Sen?
Ans. Nothing happened to her, she is still enjoying at various locations like the Maldives.

Que. Who is Anushka Sen's best friend?
Ans. Jannat Zubair is her best friend.

Que. How can I meet Anushka Sen?
Ans. You can contact her at her mail id (anushkasen0402@gmail.com) to book an appointment.

This is the full details on Anushka Sen Age, Family, Boyfriend, Biography, Net Worth & More. Share this post with your friends and keep visiting us on celebwale.com for famous personalities and trending people's biography with updated details. If you have any thoughts, experiences, or suggestions regarding this post or our website. you can feel free to share your thought with us.

Nominations

2019Indian Television Academy AwardsBest Actress - DramaJhansi Ki RaniNominated

2022Popular Actress - WebCrashhNominated

Web series

2021CrashhJia/Alia Mehra

2022SwaanngMuskaan

Music videos

YearTitleSinger(s)Ref.

2011"Humko Hai Aasha"Unknown

2019"Gal Karke"Asees Kaur

2020"Superstar"Neha Kakkar and Vibhor Parashar

"Pyar Naal"Vibhor Parashar

"Meri Hai Maa"Tarsh

"Aaina"Monali Thakur and Ranajoy Bhattacharjee

2021"Teri Aadat"Abhi Dutt

"Chura Liya"Sachet–Parampara

"Choorha"Nikk

2022"Mast Nazron Se"Jubin Nautiyal

"Is This That Feeling"Shekhar Ravjiani

Television

Year	Title	Role	Notes	Ref.
2009	Yahaan Main Ghar Ghar Kheli	Misti		[12]
2011	Devon Ke Dev...Mahadev	Child Parvati		[12]
2012–2016	Baalveer	Meher Dagli / Baal Sakhi		[13]
2018	Internet Wala Love	Diya Verma		
2019	Jhansi Ki Rani	Manikarnika "Manu" Rao/Rani Lakshmi Bai		[6]
2020	Apna Time Bhi Aayega	Rani Singh Rajawat	18 episodes	[15]
2021	Fear Factor: Khatron Ke Khiladi 11	Contestant	9th place	

Films

Year	Title	Role	Notes	Ref.
2015	Crazy Cukkad Family	Unnamed		
2019	Lihaaf: The Quilt	Young Ismat Chughtai		
	Sammaditthi	Bittu	Short film	

www.ingramcontent.com/pod-product-compliance
Lightning Source LLC
Chambersburg PA
CBHW071255140726

47996CB00007B/2857